Z

z

PARENTING PANDORA

Understanding Your Child With Reactive
Attachment Disorder

By Essie Johnson

Copyright 2014 Essie Johnson

Amazon Edition, License Notes

z

Table of Contents

z

Introduction

The story of Pandora's Box comes from a Greek myth. Pandora received a box as a wedding gift. She innocently opened it only to release the evils of the world. In the end, all that remained in the box was hope.

In 2007, my husband and I adopted a little girl who was just 4 years old. She would join our biological daughter, who was 2.

Genea was born in Ukraine and lived in an orphanage until she was adopted and brought to the United States by a couple for whom she would be their first child. She lived with them for the next two and a half years as they tried, without success, to help her.

The biggest issue, as they saw it, was that she was miserable. Severely withdrawn- except for screaming fits- she even disassociated at times. They sought help, but felt therapists and doctors blamed them. Their marriage fell apart and they began to search for another family to adopt her.

My husband and I met Genea and immediately adored her. She was happy and always excited to see us. A beautiful child, the type to elicit compliments from even the most cantankerous elder. She and our biological daughter became life -long sisters the day they met, and we proceeded with the adoption.

Following several months of visits, both families met at a fast food restaurant one last time. Genea was her usual self; bouncy, charming, happy. She was indifferent to the mother, which was normal, and their final goodbye was swift and easy.

Taking my new set of daughters home, I put them both down for a nap. I did not see that happy, delightful child again for four years.

Volcanic explosions, unending tantrums, rages at an intensity that made me wonder if a small child could cause herself an aneurism. That a tiny little girl could create this whirlwind of chaos was incomprehensible. I thought I knew exhaustion. I thought I knew frustration and I thought I knew anger. I did not. Left in the literal puddles of spit she sprayed while shrieking, was everything I thought I knew about parenting, and myself as well.

The next several years were spent trying to understand what was happening. It was like living in the Gravitron ride at a carnival. Whirling faster and faster, immobilized, plastered to the wall by centrifugal force.

Seven years later, I do not have all the answers but I have found a few. This booklet is my attempt to share what I have learned.

Chapter 1

Reactive Attachment Disorder

Reactive Attachment Disorder is a severe disruption of typical development, resulting in a child unable to bond. However, it is much more than that.

Children affected have developed extreme emotional reactions that can be extraordinarily difficult to live with, sometimes even impossible. The things they think of to do are unbelievable. The incessant mental battering and constant intensity are exhausting. They can be volatile, violent, and hateful.

At the same time, they are children. Children who have had no base to structure themselves around, and who *can* get better.

Raising a child with RAD is likely the most challenging thing most of us have ever done. Typical parenting techniques do not work. Our children might take one step forward only to regress to a point more difficult than where they started.

Despite sometimes counting the days until they turn eighteen, we love them. We want them to love us and love life. We want them to be healthy and happy. We wonder how we'll react the first time police come to our door and we pray our children don't hurt anyone besides ourselves.

This mini book contains a few of the things that have helped make things better in my family. Finding relief from the agonizing symptoms of an illness they do not deserve is the goal.

No one should have to live as they do.

Chapter 2

Predictability

I believe the driving force behind most Reactive Attachment Disordered behavior is the need to create predictable situations. The obsession with control and the compulsion to constantly manipulate circumstances reduces feelings of fear. They don't seek love to replace fear, they seek predictability to control fear.

Safety is the second tier in Maslow's Hierarchy of Needs. The first tier is physiological and includes breathing, food, sleep, and homeostasis (the unconscious drive to stay the same). When those needs are met, the person focuses on safety. Until a person feels safe, they cannot move "up" to the levels of love, self-esteem and self-actualization.

The child with RAD feels constantly unsafe. Even when they *are* safe in a stable and loving environment, the dangers that were burned into their brains from infancy are a constant buzz in the background. This could well be why love is not enough.

Children with RAD exists on only 2 planes- *now*, and *next*. The past is not relevant, it can't help them anymore. The future is equally irrelevant. They cannot worry about tomorrow when they don't know what will happen next. There is no trust that existing safety will continue. They care about what is happening right now, and what immediately follows.

When they do not know what is coming they feel anxiety that increases from minute to minute. They manipulate in order to *make* what happens next be what they *predict* will happen next.

Years ago, my daughter would come home from kindergarten and every day immediately escalate into a level 10 meltdown. Always standing in the same spot in the middle of the hallway, she began with a provoking question. For example, she might ask to be driven to the toy store. When the answer was no, she commenced with shrieking. I ignored it to see if she might calm down. She never did. I would tell her what TO do, like standard parenting experts recommend, "Calm down honey". She did not. Then came the warning- "calm down or you'll have to take a time out in your room". Wait a few more minutes (she never calmed down with the warning either), and send her to her room.

I was as consistent as possible and yet every single day was the same. Traditional parenting is dependent on consistency. Always issue a firm consequence for unwanted behavior. Any deviation will cause the behavior to repeat. But here was the complete opposite. I was being as consistent as anyone could be yet the behavior did not stop, or even slow down.

It appeared she had no sense of cause and effect. Having this tantrum every day meant going to her room. She hated going to her room. Logically, she should stop the tantrums to stay out of her room.

It's embarrassing how long it took me to realize what was happening. She was rigidly doing the same thing every day so I would issue the same consequence. She had learned cause and effect alright, just not in the traditional way. Her escalating behavior after school each day was actually a series of manipulated steps to push me to react the same way I always did- predictably. She was *causing* with her behavior *the effect* of my reactions. It was what she wanted all along.

The consequences of going to her room and having her family frustrated with her could not compare to the strength of her need to reduce the fear of what might happen otherwise.

Here lies one of the most difficult parts of having a child with RAD. Trying to use motivators or consequences to change their behavior is not likely to work. Very little is more valuable to her than feeling safe. Threatening her safety to compel a change in behavior is not just unfair, it will backfire. She will become even more scared and her behavior will be more manipulative. Additionally, once you have 'gone there', she will compulsively push you to 'go there' again- forcing the predicted reaction.

What Might Work:

Be inconsistent with problem behavior, and use rock solid consistency with behavior you want to see repeated.

Here is an example. The child is told to wipe down the kitchen table after lunch. She does, and it's an excellent job on all but one conspicuous corner. I call that the "F- you spot". If you react with a consistent response, such as pointing out the spot in an aggravated tone and having her wipe it, you have guaranteed it WILL happen every time.

Instead, create mild discomfort by changing your reaction with each opportunity. Maybe once you finish for her. Next time, sing a song about tables. Quietly ignore it. Wait for her to get cozy with a movie, then have her re- do it. Lay across the table and announce it is your new bed. Comment loudly how happy you are that there is a spot already messy so you don't have to worry about wrecking her clean table.

Incidentally, behavior that is deliberate like this can also be caused by the other driving force of RAD behavior, connection- attention. It's covered in more detail in that section.

Use rigid consistency with what you want to see repeated. Pick a complimentary phrase and repeat it without change. In the above situation, she is asked to clean the table and she does it thoroughly. Pick yourself up off the floor, it could happen. With a calm, soft voice, say your phrase.

My phrase is "wow, look at that. You're trying to surprise me with your excellence, aren't you"? Okay, it's not the most logical phrase but it came out one day and stuck. I hold up my hand and she slaps a high 5. EVERYTHING is exactly the same. I don't change my tone or my volume. Every time, I widen my eyes a little, smile in a barely-there way, and repeat myself.

I found out the hard way, excitement causes her to bubble over. She cannot handle too much of any feeling, even a happy one, and it leads to a meltdown. Making a big show of how great she is will cause a meltdown and often ensures the greatness is not repeated. We keep it pleasant and mild.

Chapter 3

Connection Attention

Alternate title:

Child, you sucked the nothing out of me 6 months ago

There are primary symptoms of RAD as listed in the DSM-V, and secondary symptoms. Most parents will scream from the rooftops, it is the incessant, exhausting, water torture behavior that will make any parent lose it. The big stuff is hard, so hard, but the relentless and unending minute to minute attention seeking is what wears you down the most.

There is no such thing as good attention or negative attention to a child with RAD. There is no distinction, there is *only attention*. It's an extremely difficult idea really grasp and personally I still struggle with it. It's like if you handed her 2 identical candy bars and label one good and the other bad. She'll want them both equally.

My theory is that those incessant jabs and provocations are her effort to connect with you. OH YES INDEEDY it is backwards and honestly, often repellent. It is designed to suck you in. She only knows that she is successful. Any attention is what she was after- it connects you with her.

Here's a bit that might be hard to stomach- the child with RAD is acting like this with you because she is attaching to you. When she is all shiny and bright in public and puts on her Miss Pretty Perfect act, it's because she does not care about those people. Part of the act is to manipulate those folks so they don't know the "real her". She saves the "real her" for you. It's a compliment. Really.   It helps to remember these are children. Little kids who have typically never had stable, positive and loving people to reinforce their inherent goodness.

She is not going to stop because it is working. She may vaguely understand that she is frustrating or annoying or angering her parent but it goes back to "no such thing as negative attention". She feels invisible. Where there is any attention she has succeeded in being noticed and increased her chances of being cared for.

As with a lot of RAD behavior, one reason it is so maddening is because there is no clear flip side. Not responding makes it worse, responding rewards the acting out- and makes it happen more.

Confront it.

When she is being disruptive for attention, let her know you see her.

"I see you and I love you".

"You are safe. I can see you".

"I always know you are there".

"I will always take care of you, everything is okay".

Label it

If she's not to a stage where she understands how she feels, start by teaching her some basic feeling words. Happy, sad, nervous, worried, scared, excited. When you see her acting in one of these ways, point it out and ask how her body feels, how her mind feels. Then label it.

Most of the time, the kids are doing these things without deliberation. It's automatic. She knows what she is doing, and usually knows it is wrong, but isn't consciously aware of making herself do it. A lecture on appropriate behavior is useless for two reasons. First, it is evidence to her that her behavior worked and second, she knows what appropriate behavior is if she does it in public.

Children with RAD have an unending desire for attention. Trying to meet the need is like trying to fill the ocean with a bucket from the dollar store. Often, when it comes to attention seeking, the behavior becomes a habit in order to get the predictable reaction. Here is a good way to give it variety and lessen the frequency.

Thanks for calling my attention to you- I need someone to take out the trash/ wash the floor/ empty the dryer.

<u>Don't Shout, Point it out</u>

Another way to manage connection attention is to disrupt the cycle by pointing it out. Attempts at manipulating a situation are useless if someone has already determined the goal.

"I hear you pretending to choke on your food. You want everyone in the restaurant ask if you are okay".

"I see you are rocking back and forth to disrupt this row of bleacher seats. You must want everyone to look at you".

No self-respecting child with RAD would ever admit their parent is right and will likely deny it. It will happen a few more times for effect, then generally is done.

When my husband left the room one day, Genea made an offhand comment that cleared up a lot. She asked, "Do you ever feel like Daddy is dead when he goes to another room? I do. It feels like he died".

She was nine. She had a constant need for attention and connection with her parents partly because when she could not see us, it felt like we were gone forever (as has happened in the past).

Chapter 4

Change

Alternate title:

She has the rest of her life scheduled to be exactly the same as yesterday.

It is usually obvious a child with RAD dislikes change. Change brings the potential for an unknown- something she cannot predict. She relies fully on her environment staying the same to feel safe.

As with many things RAD, it goes to a whole new level. Moved the soap dish? Change. Buy her a new toy? Change. Birthday coming? Change. Like attention, there is no difference between good change and bad change. Only change and it is all bad. Many a family trip to Disney has been ruined by a powerful fear of change that an autograph from Sleeping Beauty cannot override.

The ramifications of a schedule change can be far reaching. There is the pre- change meltdown and the post- change meltdown. Additionally though, if the change does not repeat, that can lead to further disruption. So if there was a surprise school assembly on Tuesday at 11:00, the following Tuesday at 11:00 will be a problem because the schedule returned to normal. It changed back. 11:00 on Tuesdays may be suspect for a while.

Change is one of the most common triggers for a child with RAD. If there is a sudden jump in meltdowns, often the reason goes back to something she could not control. It changed without her permission (which she would never give). A substitute teacher, a cheeseburger on Hamburger Tuesday, or the mail coming late.

Unfortunately, no one can control change. It can help to confront that with her. Whether she engages in *fill in the blank* or not, the change is still going to happen. She might get in trouble, she might anger people, she might lose friends, but she cannot stop the change from happening. When it's something that has already happened, commiserate with her. It doesn't matter if it seems silly, it rocked her little world. Talk about the horrible things that could have gone wrong, then point out none it happened because you take care of her.

Many specialists recommend scheduling the day. In our situation, a schedule resulted in extreme opposition and defiance- leading to violent meltdowns. It was much more useful to structure the day around repeating events.

Structure is more about passive events happening in a predictable way, using one event to indicate time for the next. Breakfast, brush teeth, get dressed. PBS TV shows until after Sid the Science Kid, then lunch, then the park.

Ritualizing structured activities helps immensely. The child with RAD is NOT a fan of variety. Dinner is at 6:00. Not 6:01 and certainly not 5:59. At dinner, she makes the drinks with hers in a blue cup and her sisters in a green cup. When there is tomato soup, cheese is always put out. Everyone gets a turn to tell about their day, in the same order.

When an unavoidable change is coming, prepare her ahead of time. Only a day, or even a few hours before it happens because telling her too early will cause her to marinate in anxiety. Let her know exactly what is happening and when- no detail is too small. It is especially important to be sure she knows everything will go back to normal afterwards. Ask what would help her feel more comfortable. It can be surprising how insightful kids with RAD are.

My daughter struggled mightily in restaurants. It was so bad that we rarely went out to eat. It was strange though, that an activity centered on one of her favorite things –a meal- was causing her to act out so intensely. One night, we had decided to go out to eat and I sat her down before we left. I itemized the usual problems she had and asked her how we could help her feel better so she did not need to do those things. She said, she did not know why she felt so scared in a restaurant but she noticed another time that she was less anxious sitting on the inside of a booth. Maybe being contained makes her feel safe, I'm still not sure. Regardless, she was right and as long as she's in the corner of a booth, she is fine.

Chapter 5

Why Typical Parenting Does Not Work

Alternate Title Courtesy of Bob Dylan: "When you ain't got nothin' you got nothin' to lose".

We hear it all the time. "Have you tried *fill in the blank with popular parenting technique du jour*"? Spanking, timing out, and of course the beloved sticker chart.

Gritting my teeth and forcing a smile reminiscent of a scary clown peering out from a sewer grate, I *want* to say "of course I tried all those things are you stupid or is it me because OF COURSE I tried all the **obvious easy** ways but none of it worked because this is all stone cold crazy!!! Eleventy!!!"

What I really say is, "yes *sigh*, I tried it *sigh*, and no, it didn't work. *Sigh*".

But why? That's the question that drove me into obsession. If I could figure out why typical parenting wasn't working, I could figure out what to do instead (I thought, anyway).

Taking Away Her Toys/ Electronics/ Etc.

This does not work because *she has already lost everything*. She has lost her country, her first family, her familiar foods, her roots, her home. How is removing a stuffed puppy from her possession going to make a dent in comparison to what she has already lost?

(Not to mention, if she is actually attached to something and cares about it, do you really want to mess that up by taking it?)

Spanking

The typical child has trust in her parents. While spanking is not a great technique for any child, typical children will recover quickly because their bond with their parent is air tight. That child knows her parents love her and will take care of her.

A child with RAD does not trust that adults will care for her and keep her safe- no matter how long the parent has been doing just that. Spanking is painful. She cannot trust a person who hurts her therefore will not be able to attach. Spanking will set the relationship back to the beginning. Or worse.

Ignore what you don't want repeated/ Ignore the negative

This is easy with a typical child. Banging on the table? Ignore it. She stops and the parent redirects to something better and praises her.

In my experience, the child with RAD **never** gives up. They will raise the stakes until they are causing damage and parents are forced to step in for safety reasons. Ignoring doesn't work partly because it puts her in a full blown panic.

The child with RAD panics because she **needs** you to see her. She does not exist if no one sees her. Former caretakers consistently ignored basic needs as well as the child herself. Her purpose, as misaligned as it is, is to connect with your attention at any cost.

Love and Logic

This book, written by Foster Cline and Jim Fay, is brilliant for the typical child. A child with RAD has not developed a system of logic that responds to loving guidance. Her logic developed in response to trauma.

Sticker Charts

Ah, the Great and Glorious Sticker Chart. Solution to every known issue on the planet. Any reward based system will fail because of the predictability factor.

How many times has your child complied perfectly with the rules to earn a reward only to blow it at the last minute? It doesn't matter how orderly and reliable her current parents are, her world is still chaotic. In her chaotic world, she cannot be 100% certain the reward will come. Whether it's because she makes a mistake or something happens that she cannot control, she does not trust the unknown. So she forces an outcome. She takes control of the result by manipulating. Since she knows she will not get the reward if she does not follow the rules, she makes certain by her behavior that it happens that way.

It's often called Self Sabotage. She may desperately want the reward. She may have been begging for the reward for ages. Unfortunately the reward will rarely be stronger than her need to feel safe.

Grounding

The basis of "grounding" is different amongst parents. Some take away the phone or TV. For others, grounding means staying in the house, a loss of freedom. It might be that a special event is taken off the calendar. Regardless, grounding usually means taking something away.

For a child with RAD, the parent simply cannot take away more than she has already lost. It also goes back to the two states of existence- now, and next. She likely does not understand time frames. In addition, children with RAD do not necessarily want freedom, it's too unpredictable.

Yelling

Yelling at a child with RAD increases their already sky- high anxiety and makes their behavior worse.

Children with RAD are sometimes described as having no 1-9. Just 10, with 10 being the most disregulated and out of control. Yelling escalates their anxiety which leads to meltdowns. She's not going to do what she was refusing, she's going to explode instead.

I used to say, my daughter *wakes up* at an 8, leaving very little margin for ordinary frustration.

"Catch them being good"

How long do you think I'm going to live?

JUST KIDDING!

This is based in the assumption that the parent will ignore them being "not good". It won't work because ignoring won't work.

Additionally, children with RAD often cannot handle compliments. It alters their homeostasis, they cannot stand it. Feeling good does not feel good, it feels different. Compliments for positive behavior will usually ensure it is never repeated. In fact, the child will often do the opposite to create predictability- now she knows what to do- and use it to ensnare connection-attention. Try instead to compliment the result, such as "wow, this room looks really nice".

My daughter was impressive with her winter accessories. She never misplaced so much as a mitten - quite the feat for 7 year old in a large elementary school. I began complimenting her on it, and by the end of a week she had "lost" all of it, piece by piece.

Chapter 6

Lying

There are a few things a parent can do almost nothing about. You cannot control bodily eliminations, you cannot control food intake, and you cannot control lying. There are however, some things a parent can do to manage lying.

Lying for a child with RAD is like receiving a million dollars with a double scoop of ice cream on top. She will lie when the truth would excuse her. She lies consistently through the day about tiny irrelevant things and she gets away with much of it. The motivation to lie and the consistent reinforcement lies receive are far stronger than any punishment or consequence that can be given.

<u>What does not work:</u>

Soap or hot sauce in the mouth

Threatening

Asking "Did you do this"?

Soap or hot sauce are aggressive. The children with RAD need to trust you will not hurt them. She cannot trust the person who does these things to her.

Threatening a child who has lied (*you better tell me or you will be grounded*) is a clear signal that they have power over you. The parent wants something and the child has total control as to whether or not to give it. As petty as it seems to an adult, to the child it is glorious.

She'll usually lie about her lies to answer any questions. Asking "why" or "did you do this" just reminds her she is in charge and she's not about to give up her control.

All kids lie. All adults lied as children and we still lie to this day. Only we call it being polite. I remember the first lie I ever told, at maybe 4 years old, to my Aunt. She usually had bright orange hair that stuck up in tufts. I loved that crazy hair!   One

day she wore a short, gray, curly wig and a
me if I liked it.

I said yes, I did.

I promptly ran to my mother to confess my sin and
she explained "white lies" to me. The distinction
was too much for my concrete little brain and it
became my passport.

Children with RAD lie for some of the same
reasons other kids do. They do not want to get in
trouble. Among friends, they think the lie will
make them look better, more interesting.

But RAD lies, dang. It's amazing and bizarre how
ridiculous the lies get! Because they CAN, and
often no one will know, it gives them the power of
the leader of the free world.

In the words of an adult recovering from RAD, "I
lied because I could and because I didn't care. I
didn't care about the people I was lying to and I
didn't care about what would happen when they
found out." But the most revealing thing she said,
and she may not have even realized it, was "I lied
because then no one could know the real me".

AHA! And there we have the crux of the disorder. If
people don't know you, they cannot attach to **you.**
If they try, they are attaching to a **character** you
made up.

Her suggestion is to never ever get in the way of
natural consequences. Let it rain.

Idea's for Lying

Parents of kids with RAD have to be creative. Thinking outside the box is a cliché, but we have to go far beyond that. Stomp the box to shreds. Set it on fire.

When your child lies, there are a few tricks. One is to fully participate in the lie when it's a crazy lie for the attention of others. Just jump on in and tell the checkout cashier about your days as a stripper. This will surprise and disorient her, and she will be uncomfortable.

Alternately, feed the skill. Are the lies logical? Are they interesting? Have her take a creative writing class or seek one out on the internet and write that story down. For whatever reason, many kids with RAD do not like writing and it will cause her discomfort. Or, she will develop writing and imagination building skills that will benefit her.

Are the lies not that good but delivered with the pure sincerity of fresh, clear, spring water? Acting classes. Channel the lies, put them in an appropriate place.

When you know she lied

Give her a 1 minute chance to be truthful. If she does she will get a break. Kids are impulsive and often say the first thing they think up. Sometimes that extra minute to process can work.

If it does, be sure to tell her what the consequence would have been had she continued to lie, and compare it to the consequence you use. Feel free to drama up a little. Such as "if you had kept lying you would have had to mow the lawn. And the neighbors too. Since you told the truth, I want you to sweep the porch". That's if you use consequences.

One of the hardest things I had to do as a parent was to stick to that! My eyeballs were sweating with frustration and nearly blew out. Very much a case of opposite parenting- oh I wanted to punish lying until the day people could live on Mars.

Give a Lying Penalty

If the things coming out of her mouth are not true, she needs her parent to help her get enough quiet time to consider what she is going to say. Additionally, if lies are coming out, her words are meaningless and therefore pointless.   No talking for 30 minutes. Any breaking of it results in 5 more minutes. This works for parents because you get some peace and quiet as well as a break from the lying.

Make it work for you

I let my daughter with RAD lie at first. Yes I did. I let it flow and watched her closely, never letting on I knew.

In the game of poker they say everyone, even the most practiced high roller, has a "tell". A microscopic physical reaction when they are bluffing. If another player can figure it out, that player will win.

Now it happens that I was a prolific and skilled liar as a kid. Having been such, I can usually tell where the child is going with their pant load. I weave her along, add prompts, give suggestions and back her straight into a corner. Trapped like a mouse.

Watching closely, a few things became noticeable. First was her dead steady eye contact. This was a kid who used eye contact to be disrespectful or oppositional, never in a positive way. When she lied, her eye contact almost blistered my corneas it was so intense, and her pupils were dilated. The rest of her face was as solid and unmoving as a granite countertop. The other thing she did was tilt her head to the left. Once her "tells" were identified it became obvious when she was lying.

I was reading a popular aggregate site when I came across this gem. Set the child up with a "tell". An example might be to say "I always know when you lie because your top lip bunches up". Then watch her try to cover her lip or keep it stick straight. Now you know.

Chapter 7

Voluntary Incontinence

Urine in places other than the toilet. My daughter frequently expresses herself with pee and it is almost a hallmark for kids with RAD.

I'll start by saying this- my daughter has been with us seven years now and it is still a problem. Obviously, I have no solution. However, I have some insights and tricks for minimizing the issue as well as ways to protect my car, furniture, self and others from it.

So, the basics. There are two issues involving urination that does not occur in a toilet. Incontinence is basically "awake peeing". Enuresis is night-time peeing, in other words, bed wetting.

They are two different issues. Fun Fact: *encopresis* is pooping outside of a toilet or other poop designated receptacle. Lots of causes for all of the above. Physical, psychological, often sexual abuse. What I am going to cover is deliberate peeing.

"Why? Why? WHY? Sweet mother of tequila is there nothing I can do to stop this peeing"? To my knowledge, no there is not. Hopefully that makes you feel better.

There are a few theories about the frequency of pee and the RAD mind. It's to push people away and/ or it's about control. These are true, according to my daughter. However, I have my own theory about its origin and why it is such an unending, stubborn issue.

Neglected children are rarely touched. An infant in an eastern European orphanage for example, is left in a crib. That's it. The crib. Even for feeding, a bottle is propped up by the rails and no one ever touches this child.

That baby pees and the warmth spreads around them. It is the only warmth they feel and it's lovely. Nobody talks to the baby. No one makes eye contact. Other babies are inches away but unreachable. Forget smiling or hanging onto a finger or playful interactions. There's not anything in the crib other than bedding. Not even a toy to curl your tiny fingers around. That comforting warm feeling from fresh urine is gone and it's now cold and wet.

Maybe a few times a day, maybe less, someone comes. They still don't look at you or talk to you but they touch you to change the diaper. If you are a lucky baby the touch is gentle and kind but even if it is cold and rough it is still the only connection you get. And you are finally dry and warm again.

The example is of an institutionalized child but the same goes for a child in standard foster care. Children are removed from biological parents in America most commonly for neglect. Even the most crack-addled, neglectful and abusive parent will eventually change a diaper that stinks.

There are probably thousands of books that address potty training children. The issue of pee in a child with RAD is NOT potty training. Mine knew darn good and well how to use a toilet. That didn't stop me though- I probably bought half the books available and tried every possibility. And made some stuff up too- like the placebo pill (a vitamin) that miraculously made pee go in the potty (it didn't).

Here's an example of the level of control she has always had over it.

Among my many thousands of mistakes was this. She was flooding pants regularly, but sometimes would have an accident (I still thought they were accidents) of a few drops. So I encouraged the drops- obviously with NO knowledge I was doing it.

I was trying to be kind, to consider she was just a scared little kid. To understand no one is perfect and all kids have a few pee accidents. I told her that I didn't care about a few drops in her underwear. No really, I told her that.

Little kids have accidents! It's okay!

I probably should have known when she tried to pin me down as to *how often* it was okay. 2 times? Once a day? Well at least I remembered it later as I put the pieces together. The pieces being, she developed a new pee issue. A few drops at a time- all day long.

Now that she is older and has a great psychologist we have learned some incredible information directly from the source.

There are many times I've had to struggle to wrap my brains around her process of logic. Although it makes no sense to me, I can follow the words she utters in a line from point (a) to point (b). This is one of those times that I had to accept it at face value.

The way she saw it, the pee brought me to her and ensured I would not leave her. She always achieved some response, even if just a neutral toned "go change your clothes".

If I failed to notice, she made sure it was unmistakable by hovering close, asking me to button her pants or leaving stains on the furniture.

In her mind, peeing on herself showed me that she needed me. If she needed me, I would not leave her.

Step away and get a tissue if you need one. Seriously.

Fear of abandonment is pervasive in RAD. Her skill at sucking me in is amazing and she could usually force me to be involved in some way. Maybe I had to get her a towel to clean up. Maybe get the vinegar out for her to wash the clothes. Maybe it was just the fact that I noticed it. And so her goal was always met. Peeing always worked to get her what she wanted.

Sticker charts and other reward systems will not work. There is not a sticker in the world big enough to cover the core issues.

The other breakthrough recently on the great subject of urination has been different. Because many times, she would pee on herself away from me.

She had begun peeing herself at her adored after school activity when there was a short break between classes. During that time, another child would act up. She seemed to want to be Genea's friend so she constantly provoked and poked at her to get her attention.

(ahem, sound familiar?)

Genea's best efforts at keeping this girl away did not work. She asked the girl to stop. Begged her. The other girl did outrageous, obnoxious and even dangerous things. This reinforced to Genea over and over, *she could not make it stop.* The kid came at her like an emaciated mosquito.

Things got overwhelming and she had no way to deal with it. So she peed. Her psychologist calls it "spraying". As in, she sprays the air with pee smell to make people go away.

Pee Management

There was a time when peeing at school was an issue. Diapers and diaper style underwear are frowned on for a child capable of using a toilet. The idea behind the school's thinking is that it's behavioral. It's a choice and she will stop when the social consequences start.

She did not. I struggled mightily with the decision but eventually sent her to school in a discrete diaper. I could not let the rotten judgment of a mentally ill child stigmatized her entire school career. Kids remember this stuff and use it in nasty little ways forever.

At home, when there is a peeing streak, the pee-er is not allowed to sit on any fabric furniture. She may sit on the floor, however, if the pee continues she has to sit on a piece of plastic. The plastic goes with her everywhere, especially in the car, and she is expected to always have it with her.

When she "forgets" her plastic, she does jumping jacks to help her memory with bilateral physical activity.

The lid on one of those plastic or rubber tote bins works beautifully. Somehow there are usually more lids than bins anyway.

She is responsible for all the clothes and furniture affected, and she cleans it all with as little input as possible.

There is one unusual idea that works fairly well. I have to shout however; NEVER EVER do this with a kid who has survived sexual abuse. Even if there is a possibility of sexual abuse, DO NOT. You will lose your child's trust forever, and likely damage her beyond repair.

If the child is a persistent day time pee-er, take away their underwear and put them in loose fitting pants. They will despise the uncontrollable feeling of urine going down their legs.

When I initially thought of this, I recoiled from myself. It seemed outright mean. However, underwear is not a right. In fact, humans were without underwear until the last century or so.

In her words, "sometimes I want to be left alone and so I pee to make people go away. But I want them to be by me. So?"

Right-o kid. So? Is a darn good question.

Chapter 8 It is not your Fault

Alternate Title: I could throw a rock at the crowd outside a super-max prison on release day and whoever the rock hit would be a better parent for this child than I.

Repeat these words:

*It's not about me, it's not about me, it **really** is **not** about me.*

Yes, it's directed at you. Yes, you are the target. Actions of the child are specifically designed to cause you the maximum frustration. And these kids are immensely successful.

It's not about me

She will hurl the most horrible combination of words ever heard. "I hate you" is a benign starting point. Comments to the effect of *you suck, you're not my real mother,* and *fuck you,* should all be considered noise. Sounds. Sounds that mean she is frustrated, scared, worried or upset.

She is trying to make her outsides match her insides. (If it works, the damage to her brain does not improve).

It's not about me

Research has shown that the brains of children who experienced neglect are actually smaller. Scans show that area's which should be activated are not, and vice versa.

One study showed teenagers with RAD are slower and less accurate when deciphering the facial expressions of others.

Another study showed a significant increase in predisposition to physical and mental medical problems.

Their brains have been damaged.

Depending on their age and severity of neglect, their bodies may not produce enough oxytocin to bond.

Their bodies over-produced cortisol in response to their early lives. Over time, it burns out and they become less responsive to concerns.

It's not about me

Decades of poverty, multiple generations of mental illness, malnutrition, exposure to toxins. Sexual, emotional, physical abuse. Neglect. Pre-natal stress and little or no pre-natal care. Multiple traumas caused by people other than you.

The brain can repair- that IS about you, but the damage already done is not.

It's not about me

It feels like it is about you for sure. That's because you are the only person left standing. It's aimed at you because you care.

You held out your hands and accepted the puzzle that is your child. It's a puzzle made up of 1000 pieces. The picture on the box does not match what is inside.   There are missing pieces, but also the pieces of a dozen other puzzles mixed in. It is impossible to put the whole puzzle together as it was new. Some pieces will never be found.

My family adopted a cat. About 2 years old, the cat took a liking to my daughter with Reactive Attachment Disorder, and vice versa. It was amazing to see and magical to watch. But here's the thing- when the cat was attaching to my daughter, she did some of the same things she did with me when I was trying to attach with her. TO THE CAT.

It is not about you.

Chapter 9 Recommendations

READ

Start with "Beyond Consequences, Logic and Control" by Heather Forbes and Bryan Post. It's about building a relationship with the child first and foremost, before worrying about consequences and such. The techniques are excellent for getting to what is causing the child's behavior, and bonding with her instead of fighting against her.

Then read "When Love is not Enough" by Nancy Thomas. The book is meant as a 'how to', and gives the best suggestions for managing problems that come up. However the most value, in my opinion, comes from her descriptions of common RAD-specific behaviors.

"The Connected Child" is excellent as well, by Karen Purvis.

"Attaching in Adoption" by Deborah Gray lays out valuable information about what 'unattached' looks like, and defines the various sub-types of RAD.

www.theaccidentalmommy.blogspot.com is my blog. Much of our history is here. The good, the bad, the ugly. Be sure to say "HI" if you stop in!

JOIN

Join an on-line support group. Many are on Facebook, search adoption or Reactive Attachment Disorder. Thankfully we don't have to rely on face to face groups in the basement of a church. We could never get to one anyway, we have a child with RAD.

There are a few groups now that do focused retreats for parents of children with traumatic backgrounds. However, even if attending one is impossible, they have a wealth of information, support and resources.

Hope Rising Website.

http://www.hoperisingforfamilies.org/ . There is a Facebook page and at least one private support group.

BeTA: Beyond Trauma and Attachment Website

http://www.momsfindhealing.com/ . A website with blog, Facebook page, and multiple support groups including one for Dads.

Attach: The Association for Treatment and Training in the Attachment of Children Website

http://www.attach.org/ . This is possibly the original organization for parents of children with attachment problems. Their Facebook presence is minimal however they put on large yearly seminars that are exceptional.

House Calls Counseling

http://www.housecallscounseling.com . They do yearly seminars for parents in Chicago, called Parenting in Space, and produced the video "Chaos to Healing". Blog and Facebook support group.

As you get into these groups, ask members for other "leads". There are incredibly helpful Facebook support groups on private pages that cannot be found otherwise.

Chapter 10 Suggestions for school

In general, let school handle school. This is an immense struggle, as most of us strongly want to be involved in the education of our children. We want to help with homework and want our kids to succeed.

When homework is an ordeal that costs peace and sanity, step away. Give her everything she needs to do it- a quiet place, an assigned time, and then back out. Most children with Reactive Attachment Disorder use homework as a wedge, or a starting point for the evening manipulations. They use it to triangulate with the teacher, to feign helplessness, or as a source for tantrums. Everything except for reinforcing what they learned at school with quiet practice at home.

Forgot homework? Let the teacher know. She can't figure out the problem? Ask the teacher tomorrow. The teacher said she doesn't have to do it? Ok! Awesome! Just zip off an email to the teacher to confirm.

Let school work be the problem of the one who should be learning. School will issue consequences. Back them up but don't re-punish. Let the school know this is how it has to be with your child. Tell them the many ways she is set up for success! Remind them then, the rest is up to her.

Author Opinion

Here's the thing. Schools are filled with dozens of professionals. They have all spent 4 years, often more, dedicated to learning the best ways to educate children. If there are 15 teachers at the school, that's 60 years of higher education. If each teacher averages 5 years in the classroom, that's 75 years of experience. Furthermore, teaching is a job. They are getting paid to help every child learn.

Let them.

Final Word

Parents often agonize over teaching their children about life.

"She has to learn she won't always get her way".

"She has to learn that people don't always get what they want".

"She has to learn life isn't fair sometimes".

Here's the deal- our children with RAD have learned those things. Their lives have not been fair. They haven't gotten what they wanted or needed. They have certainly learned to delay gratification. They learned these things under circumstances no one should have to live through. They were forced by circumstances into grossly unfair lives they did not deserve.

She already knows.

Disclaimers

I AM NOT A PROFESSIONAL in ANY area of adoption. Not in social work, not psychology, not medicine, not teaching. None of it.

I DO have a Bachelor's Degree in Communication Disorders. It has not been relevant. My daughter was able to successfully fake a speech disorder, hoodwinking me as well as professionals at school.

I DO have a lengthy background working with kids from hard places. A few decades of jobs with children with mental illness, autism, behavioral disorders, who survived abuse, and who faced down many other challenges. A group home for girls 5-12 who had been sexually abused. A grant program for at risk teenagers. A detention center for juvenile delinquents.

None of it prepared me for what moved into my home that spring day.   I learned, epic failure after epic failure.

My daughter is now 11 years old. She came to us at the age of 4. I can only speak to children between those ages.

What works for us may not work for anyone else. If it works today, it may backfire tomorrow. A technique might help manage a single area but make 5 other problems pop up in its place. Often it is a matter of choosing between options where none is ideal. If a child responds to an idea with aggression or destruction, STOP. And never, *ever*, mess with their food.

Only "stage names" have been used.

Final disclaimer. I wrote this up on my laptop. It has not been edited. Not a single professional in publishing laid eyes on it. The multitude of errors are all mine. I did my best.

Made in the USA
San Bernardino, CA
13 November 2015